Your NICU Story

Reflecting on Your Family's Experience

MAHALEY PATEL, LMFT, PMH-C
AND EMILY SOUDER, LCSW-C, PMH-C
WITH RAVI V. PATEL

Copyright © 2025 Mahaley Patel and Emily Souder

All rights reserved. No portion of this book may be reproduced in any form without permission from the publisher, except as permitted by U.S. copyright law. For permissions contact:
mahaleypateltherapy@gmail.com
emily@emilysouder.com

Visit the authors' website at www.yournicustorybook.com

This guide is not meant as a replacement for psychotherapy or working through perinatal-related topics with a professional. The reader should consult a physician or a mental health professional in matters relating to their mental health and particularly with respect to any symptoms that may require diagnosis or medical attention.

Cover and interior design by Jess Creatives

Edited by Jodi Brandon

Emily Souder author photo by Courtney Keaton
Mahaley Patel author photo by Kelsey Edwards

First Edition

ISBN-13: 978-1-7346309-3-0

DEDICATION

Mahaley
For Saachi, my child of joy. You are the best thing that has ever been mine.

Emily
For NICU Baby D. and the NICU providers who help families feel seen, cared for, and loved every day.

Contents

Authors' Notes	7
Preface	9
Introduction	15
A Letter to Our NICU Families	21
Signs	23
The Partner Experience: Ravi's Story	29
The Partner Experience: Alison's Story	41
Section 1: The Beginning	53
Section 2: The Stay	63
Section 3: Your Baby	87
Section 4: Leaving Part of You Behind	101
Section 5: Going Home	121
Resources	141
Acknowledgments	143
About the Authors	147

Authors' Notes

This space is inclusive of all readers, regardless of gender or the titles/terms you feel safest using. Use the language you feel is the best for you.

It's important to us to name our limitations. Both Emily and Mahaley are in heterosexual relationships, and we know that despite our best intentions to include LGBTQ+ folks and help them feel seen here, there may be certain pathways unintentionally left out. Please know this is unintentional and you are welcome to interchange any of our language with any of yours.

As you read this book, certain words, memories, or stories might bring up powerful feelings for you. Please be mindful of this, and take time away or request help if needed. You also have the option of skipping parts that elicit emotions that feel like too much. The Preface details one author's NICU experience and infant loss, and additional parts of this story are shared in Signs. The Partner Experience: Ravi's Story also covers a personal NICU experience and infant loss. In The Partner Experience: Alison's Story, a NICU experience and the family's experience with cancer are shared.

**

This book is not meant to replace psychotherapy or working through postpartum and/or grief-related topics with a professional. However, it can of course be used as a tool within the context of such work.

It's healthy, and so very helpful, to receive professional support if you have experienced an upsetting or traumatic medical event or a loss. Also, if you have symptoms of depression and/or anxiety, please don't hesitate to seek professional help with working through it. If you notice that journaling about your experience elicits a strong reaction that feels scary to you, don't be afraid or embarrassed to ask for help. More people have been there than you know. We've included resources at the end of the book if you're wanting or needing some support.

Preface

Mahaley

On February 2, 2023, my daughter Saachi Helen Patel was born. The pregnancy with her had gone smoothly, and my husband and I were expecting to leave the hospital as a complete family of four. Unfortunately, that is not how our story unfolded. During labor, her heart rate dipped and our providers were unable to get it back up. I was rushed into an emergency C-section and Saachi was unresponsive when she was born. After they successfully resuscitated her, they put her on a cooling blanket and transferred her to the neonatal intensive care unit (NICU). She had suffered meconium aspiration and, despite the doctors' best efforts, she died after five world-shattering days in the NICU at Monroe Carell Jr. Children's Hospital at Vanderbilt.

Her birth and her death changed the fabric of who I am and of our entire family. Over the last two years I have had to sort through a tremendous amount of grief and trauma. One of the things I kept coming back to was our time in the NICU. The sounds, the beeps, the wires, and the smells. The nurses and the doctors. The otherworldly amount of medical information we had to sort through in just five days. The medical bills, amounting to more than $350,000, and the gratitude I felt to have health insurance. And the feeling of walking out of the NICU on February 7, 2023, with empty arms.

Families whose baby or babies received care in the NICU have so much thrown their way. It can be an incredibly traumatic and overwhelming journey, and I knew I wanted to help NICU families sort through their experience, but I also knew I didn't want to do it alone. When I thought about writing a book for families in the NICU, I kept coming back to Emily's book, Birth Story Brave, which I found profoundly helpful and have used for years in working with therapy clients sorting through birth trauma. She has a way with words that I find so incredibly compassionate, inclusive, and healing. I decided to take a leap of faith and reach out to her, and I am so thankful she said yes to collaborating on this project together.

Our culture isn't always great at honoring stories that are hard, are complex, and don't have a silver lining or a happy ending. My hope with this book is that it gives you a safe space to process your NICU experience and contributes to your healing in some way.

Preface

Emily
The first time I stepped into a NICU, I was 15. Self-conscious and a bit awkward, I slipped through the doorway into the vast, dim room. My memory tells me I had on a protective gown, but that part is fuzzy. A nurse introduced me to Baby D. She showed me a wooden rocking chair. Placed the baby in my arms. And I rocked the baby. Did I talk to her? Did I smile at her? Or was I too embarrassed by being in close proximity to the nurses to take those chances? I wish I knew. Even though I can't call up those details from the murky depths of my memory, threads of something even more basic have woven through my heart all these years, leaving a name on my lips: D.

Though there were nurses in the NICU, I didn't meet any parents. I was volunteering at a large hospital in Baltimore City and was stationed on the pediatric floor. It was an interesting place for a teenager to be. A hard place, sometimes. Some days I would sit on the floor in the hospital unit playroom, creating towers from blocks or bracelets from beads with kiddos who needed a break from their hospital rooms. Other times I would visit kids unable to leave their rooms. I remember spending time with a particular little girl who enjoyed watching the city below through the big glass window in her room, her smooth, hairless head framed by the light pouring through the window. When I wasn't spending time with patients, I sometimes helped out by sanitizing the hospital unit's toys.

Something I learned during volunteering was that not all parents are able to be with their children constantly when they're in the hospital. There might be other kids at home who need care, or the parents may need to go to work. Providers and volunteers help, as they're able, to give hospitalized kiddos extra support beyond medical care. The task of a NICU volunteer? Holding babies. Rocking, cradling, caring. I can't imagine how indescribably difficult it must be for parents who need to split their time between the NICU and everywhere else. In an ideal situation, they wouldn't need to.

I'm not a NICU parent; I'm a PICU (pediatric intensive care unit) parent. As a neurodivergent mom, I have a nervous system that's already pretty sensitive. A severe medical emergency for my son pushed my system to limits it had never known before. The terrifying hours leading up to our stay, and the stay itself—though very brief and ending with our child expected to make a full recovery—live in my body to this day. Even after layers of healing, there are still more ways the experience makes itself known and offers itself up for renewed compassion and fresh understanding. That's grief, doing what it does. Its changing presence doesn't signify a personal shortcoming or a failure. It's just part of the process, and part of being human.

While I have supported NICU families in my work as a therapist, before now I have not dedicated an entire book to their stories and experiences. NICU families deserve that space and more. I believe all stories we create about our life experiences are incredibly important, and that we very rarely get the time or opportunity to become aware of the stories we're telling ourselves or each other. Mahaley and I are here specifically to make space for that together.

Introduction

We're really glad you're here. A NICU stay is often, though not always, unexpected. Time in the NICU can be a wild departure from the vision you imagined for after your baby's or babies' birth. Milestones you looked forward to are different or don't happen at all. Changing your baby into the "going home" outfit gets delayed, or you don't get the chance to even try that outfit on your little one. The new baby snuggles you pictured, if you can snuggle your baby, aren't at home with sunlight streaming through the window. They're in a dim, sterile space. Those cuddles are still so very important, and also so very different. All of these things add up. If we don't have an outlet to process these experiences—to talk about them, to share them, to hear similar stories—we can experience a stuckness. We might not even realize the things we're thinking or feeling are impacting our lives, and yet they are. How we think about ourselves, how we navigate our days, and how we feel physically—all of these and more are impacted by unprocessed experiences.

Trauma is a very real outcome for parents whose babies spend time in the NICU. Even with the best care providers, there is so much uncertainty and misalignment with "normal" life. And our friends and family members, as caring and supportive as they may be, aren't usually a place for us to unpack all of our worries and help us be with the "story" of our NICU experiences. Story work, which includes reflecting on and allowing space for all the parts of your experience to be expressed, is probably why you're reading this and why we're here together.

Too often, parents' stories about their NICU experiences get lost in the shuffle. Yes, your baby should be the center of attention when it comes to receiving care, yet the care of the family is also essential. Part of that care is creating space for families to process and sort through what they have experienced: the hard, the tough, the amazing. All of it.

Our hope with this book is to invite dads and partners to share in the reflection and processing of their experiences too. You will notice some questions throughout the book are labeled "Partner Question." Those are questions we've highlighted to acknowledge the unique experience and perspective of being the partner. With that said, all the questions in this book are for everyone, so go ahead and answer a question if it feels right for you, regardless of its label.

We also want to recognize that NICU parents are often lovingly supported by other types of caregivers such as their own parents, other family members, or

Introduction

friends. Where would we be without doulas and other caregivers who feel like family?

We know how impactful your NICU experience was. We know how it hangs on your heart and how the memories hit you square in the chest, seemingly out of nowhere. We also know there are nuances to your story. You may have experienced profound care from a provider that made you feel incredibly loved while you navigated the hardest time of your life. Creating the space for nuance, and for the unbelievably intricate details of your story, is exactly what we are doing here.

What to Expect

Let's talk about what to expect while you're finding your way through *Your NICU Story*. Before you dive into reflecting on your story, you have an opportunity to read a bit more about Mahaley's story and the symbolism of the butterfly on the book cover in Signs. You also get a chance to get a front-row seat as two different contributors share their NICU experiences from the perspective of a non-birthing partner. Ravi Patel, Mahaley's husband, shares what it was like for him to be a NICU dad, and Alison Coven, a queer mom, shares her experience as a non-birthing partner to her wife. We invite you to spend time with each of these sections and to see what lessons or information they might have to offer, even if you might not think their experience aligns with your own.

Your NICU Story

As you'll read in The Partner Experience: Ravi's Story and The Partner Experience: Alison's Story, and as you likely already know, many times dads and non-birthing partners feel lonely and forgotten in their experience of navigating the NICU with their family and while sorting through their emotions during and after the stay. We know you'll appreciate the way Ravi paints his story so vividly, while weaving humor into his tale as only he can. Alison (her name and the names of her family members have been changed) shares a captivating and heartwarming glimpse into her family's dual experience of navigating a cancer diagnosis and a NICU stay as a queer family, an experience that includes a plethora of nuances. The roles that dads and non-birthing partners step into are varying and complex in their own unique ways, and they deserve to be recognized.

The remainder of the book is divided into five sections of questions. Each section contains questions relating to a period of time or a theme relating to your NICU experience. We offer lined pages onto which you can record your responses if you'd like. Here's what to expect from each section:

Section 1: The Beginning covers the start of your story, wherever that is for your family. Here, we're easing in. We want to start off gently.

Section 2: The Stay is the section with the most questions and goes into the details and unique intricacies of your time in the NICU.

Section 3: Your Baby focuses on the development of your relationship with your baby. There are some big questions in this section that might take longer to answer. That's okay; take the time you need and know there's no rush.

Section 4: Leaving Part of You Behind is a space for parents whose baby passed away prior to leaving the NICU, but this may also be helpful for families whose baby went home on hospice care.

Section 5: Going Home invites parents who left the NICU with their baby to reflect on that experience.

You are in control of your pacing while going through this book. You don't need to rush. There will be times you might want to pause with a certain memory or topic, and that's okay. Be mindful when something feels like too much; be mindful when you're ready for more. You can step away whenever you need. We trust you will find exactly the speed that works best for you. It might feel a bit quiet right now, but you have an inner knowing. You can trust it.

Note that the length of your NICU stay doesn't change the importance/impact of your story. We know being in the NICU for days rather than weeks or months can be life-changing. We honor all of that here. Additionally, we recognize that some families have had multiple NICU experiences that may take them on different pathways throughout the book. This book is yours to choose what to engage with and what to skip.

Lastly, please don't feel limited by the amount of space we provide for writing; feel free to add sheets of paper as needed or use your own journal. There's no need to condense your story to make it fit. Give it all the space it needs. There are extra pages for writing at the end of each section. Also, if you find that your words have no trouble fitting into the provided space, that's fine too! Your story is your story. Its length doesn't make it matter more or less. Digital or voice recording options for your reflections work too!

We have been looking forward to being with you during this exploration. See what you might need with you to give yourself comfort—physically, mentally, emotionally—as you move through these pages. Check in with yourself. Are you thirsty? Do you need to take a stretch break? Would a blanket help you feel cozier? Once you have available comforts in place, turn the page.

A Letter to Our NICU Families

Dear NICU Families,

We see you. There are times when you might have felt, or you might still feel, invisible, but we see you. We see your forced strength throughout this journey. The devotion to your little one. The silent prayers. The gentle touches through plastic walls. The scribbled notes on pieces of paper, written in a frenzy to try to keep up with the doctors' updates. We understand the NICU can feel like another world. The sounds, the beeps, the monitors, the doctors' rounds, and the waiting. And, for some, an ending that changes your life forever.

We're grateful you will be spending time with your NICU story, because we know how much it has affected your life. Thank you for letting us join you on this path. Your story and your baby's story have lots of space here. And yet, this book doesn't need to be the end of your exploration if you don't want it to be. There are lots of ways to experiment with expressing your feelings, including art, music, advocacy, and movement. Going to therapy is also a great way to explore how you want to express yourself. Your creativity might take you places you can't possibly imagine. It's okay to keep the momentum going if that feels right to you. There may also be times when you just want to take it slow, and those are times when rest is productive. You will be given many opportunities for growth; don't be afraid to listen when they speak to you.

    With deep caring,
    Mahaley and Emily

Signs

Mahaley

A few days after leaving the NICU, I became desperate for Saachi to send me a sign. Something. Anything. A signal to me that one, she made it to "the other side," and two, she was going to find a way back to me. I needed her. One of my closest friends is an incredibly gifted medium. "She will send you a sign when she feels you are ready for one," Shannon assured me. If I'm being honest, I was frustrated. I wanted one right then and there. But I decided to have faith in my daughter—a faith that has only strengthened over the last two years.

A month after Saachi's death, my best friend of 20 years, Holland, came to visit. She took the lead on taking my oldest daughter, Amelie, who was six at the time, for outings so I could rest. One afternoon they found their way into a local shop in Franklin, Tennessee, full of handcrafted art inspired by nature. The shop owner took a liking to my daughter. Unprompted, he came over and handed her a real framed butterfly from his shop. He started telling her about butterflies, how their life is short but meaningful, and also how they connect us. Holland

and Amelie brought the framed butterfly home, and I happened to look at the bottom of the frame. The butterfly was named "Morpho Rhetenor Helena." Saachi's middle name is Helen (after my late grandmother). My husband and I long debated using Helen or Helena for her middle name. This was my first sign.

Butterflies have remained a significant part of our story. Friends and strangers who have heard our story have sent me butterfly pictures from all over the world. When we took my son, Kaaya, for his first walk after he was born, six butterflies swarmed us on our walk. Two butterflies stayed on the stroller the entire time. On Saachi's first birthday we did a butterfly release, which is now our yearly tradition. (Thank you, Kara, for the idea). And a butterfly stayed with my daughter Amelie for two entire hours. It would fly away and then come back to her. I wouldn't have believed it if I hadn't seen it with my own eyes. Saachi did, indeed, find her way back to us.

When thinking about the cover art for this book, the only thing that ever felt right was a butterfly. Butterflies signify many things to different people. Their life is brief, but beautiful and meaningful. My daughter's life was brief. But she is still creating magic and meaning all around. Maybe butterflies resonate with you and maybe they do not. I hope, at the very least, they help you see the possibility of beauty around your baby and their story, whether they are living or not.

Your NICU Story

A Butterfly Poem

A butterfly flutters its wings
In the crisp morning air
I can see it in the garden
Fragile and weightless and beautiful
It rests where the roses bloom
Where your hands would've reached

It does not stay long
A moment—a breath
Then gone, as if it was never there
But I saw it
I know it was real

Just like you
Who came to me in the morning
Fragile and weightless and beautiful
Then gone, as if you were never there
But I saw you
I know it was real

Butterflies do not live long
Their life is brief and they were never meant to stay
Carried out by the same air that brought them in
A baby, carried out in her mother's arms
The same arms that brought her in

Signs

The air still moves where you were
My arms still remember your weight
And when the butterfly returns,
I do not chase it
I just watch,
And whisper your name

– Mahaley Patel

The Partner Experience: Ravi's Story

Written by Ravi V. Patel

I am Mahaley's husband. In years past I would have said, "Mahaley is my wife." But, I've since learned that I am not number one in the executive suite. She would tell you that I am, in fact, number seven, behind her, our three living children, our two annoying cats, and our sweet angel, Saachi.

I was asked to write something that might represent the "hetero-normative male perspective" (which I qualified for simply by not understanding the term), but I have bad news: No male is going to get anywhere near this book. You already know this. We don't read the books. We are asked to read them. We say we will read them. We put the books on our nightstand because we mean to read them. But then, we don't read them. At this very moment, I have 10 books next to my bed that I'm behind on not reading.

Likelier than not, a woman is reading this on behalf of a man. It shouldn't have to be this way, though it so often is. I'll try to do my best to impart whatever wisdom I can to help you help this man. And if you are somehow able to get this man to read this section of the book, I make this one commitment: I'll keep it as brief as possible, because we men also often have short attention spans, and it will be good for both of you.

The day Saachi was born was the worst day of my life, a close second to which were the five days after, which culminated in her death. I still regularly have visions from those days, perhaps most often is the memory of holding my wife's hand as she screamed while they rushed to open her up—I thought I was losing her and the baby—and then trying to hide any expression from my face as I saw them lift a lifeless baby from the other side of that blanket they put up between her and and the operation (as if that would somehow shield her from the very obvious panic of everyone in the room). I don't think I'll ever stop seeing that moment, but I have a terrible memory, so I remain hopeful.

Those five days changed us both forever.

My trauma is completely different from my wife's.

She experienced the physical stress of many rounds of IVF, followed by nine months of pregnancy on the unpleasant side (I'll never understand women who love being pregnant, and also never understand the rest of women), and then of course an emergency C-section that resulted in the loss of the baby she'd

The Partner's Experience: Ravi's Story

carried that whole time. In the days and months after we lost Saachi, her trauma took the form of grief and loss. My wife's trauma is mainly the loss of an expectation she had held for nine months: saying goodbye to Saachi without getting to say hello.

It was five days that changed us both forever, but I realize now that this moment highlighted two very different coping mechanisms.

Mahaley felt she had barely survived the loss of her daughter and a massive attack on her mind and body. Her coping mechanism was to go inward. She was trying to feel and understand her pain as deeply as possible, and trying to honor Saachi as best as she could.

I skipped all of that, and went straight to *What do I need to do? Who do I need to call? How can I make sure my family will be okay?* It was a job. I cannot explain why, but I was so focused. My trauma has more to do with the experience of managing the loss, and how it impacted my family, and trying to thrust us forward day to day; I was in charge. If Mahaley's trauma was more about loss and damage, mine was more about barely surviving the front lines of a war.

But also, I didn't really have a choice at first. My wife was fresh out of surgery, barely awake, and emotionally paralyzed. She needed to heal. I had to approve everything they did to Saachi from the moment she was resuscitated (11 minutes after they started performing CPR), or at least attempt to make sense of a bunch of stuff doctors explained to me. And over the next five days, all I kept thinking was how much harder this must be for someone who can't even think straight. I felt lucky that I was focused. So many meetings with so many doctors. So many departments, and processes, scenarios, and big decisions.

Perhaps the biggest decision Mahaley and I made very early on was that we wanted the hospital to let us know as soon as they had real information on Saachi's brain damage. If it looked like our dear girl had no real hope to live a happy life, we didn't want to make her suffer any longer than she needed to. And so, we pushed very hard to get to the point of receiving a full brain scan—which finally arrived on day five—as soon as possible.

Multiple times a day, I would wheel Mahaley around from her side of the hospital to Saachi's for a visit, and in between we would attend meetings with doctors and nurses. By the way, why are hospitals so fucking depressing? Don't they know we are already depressed? Can we get a plant in here? But, thank god for the people in that building, who I now have come to respect on an entirely new level. From the doctors to nurses, these people were working so hard to help us in every way, and leading with their hearts. I have come to hate people who complain about hospital

The Partner's Experience: Ravi's Story

workers as if they are restaurant servers; these people are heroes and deserve all the love and respect in the world.

Anyway, without a doubt the most beautiful part of the worst days in our lives was the community that showed up for us. Close friends, but also people we barely knew, showed up like heroes. Everyone came to our rescue, from all the Indian doctors I know, to Facebook friends who connected us with friends who had gone through similar situations. By far, this was the best thing that happened to us: finding other people who had been through it.

Then there was the administrative part of just updating people—this is a really taxing part of the job that nobody talks about—and also helping them cope when they inevitably want to share a cry with you; it was always so touching, but also just another very taxing part of the job. At night, I would lie next to Mahaley till she fell asleep, then try to fall asleep on the sofa, and instead start researching various medical terms and scenarios I had learned that day, then asking more questions to my various Indian doctor friends. I also journaled and started a Google Doc that was essentially a business plan for my life, which I had started to rewrite with this current incident as our "inciting incident."

Then there was our six-year-old daughter, who had not yet met Saachi because she said she was too scared to meet her until she got better. Amelie's grandparents were watching her while we were in the hospital, but on day four when the writing was on the wall, I went home to tuck her in. I had a plan. I intentionally cried (it wasn't hard, but I wanted to model the pain), telling her how scared I was for Saachi, and she cried with me. I told her how Mom and I were going to this thing called therapy to help us understand our feelings better. I told her that I understood her being afraid to see Saachi before she was well, but I was afraid that if we did somehow end up losing Saachi, that Amelie might go the rest of her life regretting not meeting her. Amelie and I cried together in silence for a few more minutes. Then she wiped her tears, took a big breath, and said, "I want to meet Saachi, and I want to try therapy." My god, is there anything better than realizing your child is way tougher than you thought?

The next day, we had the big meeting with all the doctors—the meeting where the MRI confirmed that most of Saachi's entire brain was damaged, and the meeting where Mahaley and I decided to remove care as soon as possible. But first, we'd have to let Amelie meet her, and then we had to tell her. I picked up Amelie from school an hour later, and we spent together what were the most beautiful and heartbreaking two hours of my life. Amelie held Saachi's hand and she read stories to her. We did art

The Partner's Experience: Ravi's Story

together, and made molds of her feet and hands. Amelie kept whispering to her little sister, "Come on, little sister, I know you can do this." She still thought that there was a chance. Afterward, we took her to the "family" room, and I told her, "The doctors just called me to speak with them. I think they have an answer on how Saachi's brain is doing." I walked outside, closed the door, waited for two minutes, then walked back in, and told her that her sister was dying.

Amelie said her goodbyes to Saachi and went home with her grandparents. Over the next few hours, Mahaley and I sat with Saachi as she passed. We listened to a playlist we had made for her. The whole time, I was mostly trying to comfort Mahaley as she cradled Saachi in arms. I barely held her, because I knew that Mahaley couldn't let her go. I was smiling and comforting, but on the inside making a plan for what to do next.

So there's a bunch of bullshit we kept dealing with after that: medical, financial, more meetings, and accepting the endless deliveries of thoughtful gifts. So many treats, toys, letters, books, religious materials for gods we now knew must not exist. It was another job just accepting these gifts, figuring out where to put them, and then finding people to take the food we could never finish before it spoiled. I felt like I was running an Amazon fulfillment center. So many sugary treats—for which now more than ever I had no resistance—as if people intuit that the solution to grief is at least partially on the same road to diabetes. But overall, it was just a lot of love that we received—love that gave us small glimmers of light in an otherwise entirely dark space.

From the first day, I made the decision that if I were to take my job seriously, the one thing I knew I could control was my instrument—my body. So, not eating the cupcakes. I'm going to be healthy, and I'm just going to try to do as many good things for myself each day as possible. At first, it was really just getting myself to keep moving and go on walks, and call friends. I tried to get Mahaley out of bed as much as possible, making the sun hit her face. This was enough of a win every day to start. That and just constant togetherness. It got boring to be honest. We didn't feel like watching anything. We had been sent all these books about grief, but that's the last thing you want to do when your brain is broken from trauma. Mahaley, always working and seeking, even at her lowest and despite being broken, read all the books. Mahaley had the books. For me, I just felt lucky that I had a wife and daughter to worry about. If I didn't have this job, I might never have left the bed.

I think the only thing you can do for a long time is keep getting up, trying to move around, trying to find small wins, and being around the people you love. That's the medicine. That, and time.

The Partner's Experience: Ravi's Story

A few weeks in, Mahaley told me that the only things that might make her feel okay were 1) doing something purposeful in Saachi's name (like a book or non-profit) and 2) another baby. So, then I started those jobs too.

And then one day I did start reading, and I came upon life-altering wisdom in a book called *Letters to a Young Poet*: Our greatest art comes from our deepest, darkest moments, but the only way to find that art is to not turn away from the darkness, but instead turn toward it. I took Mahaley to lunch a couple days later and read the excerpt to her. I said, "This is the beginning of our comeback. If we want to do something purposeful, let's figure out a way to share our story, because that's how we can dig deeper in the darkness, understand our own experience better, and maybe help others who might otherwise feel alone." That's why Mahaley now specializes in grief and loss, and it's why she's written this book. She's an impressive woman, isn't she?

So, my advice to any partner in my position:

1. Do therapy, ideally couples' therapy. It's like a board meeting for your life, and you need to track your goals in life right now more than ever.
2. Go for walks and call your friends even when you don't want to.

3. Get sunlight every day, and make sure your partner does the same.
4. Hang out with your family as much as possible; that's the medicine.
5. Your greatest loss is also your greatest opportunity, so know that the deep hole you feel is also going to be the source of your greatest potential, whenever you're ready to go to work.

While I haven't been journaling as much as I did in those first few months, I still do it frequently, adding any constructive thoughts or ideas to said Google Doc, a life business plan for which the mission is living a fun and purposeful life. I know it's a bit weird to do these things, but I feel more grounded and focused when I treat my life like a business, as I think running a family is the most important business we will ever run, despite it only losing money. It helps me create clear goals, and track the plan. Like any business plan, it starts with a clear mission.

Whether you know it or not, we are all writing our life story. As life does, many chapters write themselves unexpectedly, and in cases like these, the story requires a rewrite. In order to look forward, you need to be able to look back. And that's why a book like this one is so meaningful. I wish you so much strength and love in whatever brought you to this book. The more you do the work, the more control you'll feel in writing the rest of your life story.

Thank you, Mahaley and Emily. For letting me be a small part of this beautiful journey. For reading all the books, for making me read some of them, for forgiving me when I don't, and for bringing this new one to all who don't yet know how much it will change their lives.

The Partner Experience: Alison's Story

Written by Alison Coven

I use the word *queer* to describe myself and our family. It's the word I reach for most when trying to encompass the vastness of the LGBTQIA alphabet soup. If it isn't your word, I hope that doesn't deter you from feeling welcome here—from feeling at home in this story. My hope is that this narrative offers resonance, even if the language isn't your own. This story is for all of us building families outside the lines, for those of us translating our lives into a language that too often defaults to something else.

If you're queer, you've likely done this kind of translation before. Chances are you're already well-practiced in transforming conventional narratives into something that fits your lived experience. You've become an expert in adapting systems that weren't designed with you in mind. I'm deeply grateful to Mahaley and Emily for giving me the opportunity to tell this story—a story that I hope offers something a little different, something honest and deeply queer.

My name is Alison. I'm a cis, white, queer woman in my late 30s—an epidemiologist by training, a bioinformatician by practice, and a mother made through hope and persistence. I'm married to Taylor, a gender nonconforming, masculine-of-center woman, and the love of my life. She is a critical-care physician-scientist, brilliant, courageous, and unwavering, who built her career caring for the critically ill.

I've wanted to be a mother for as long as I can remember, though infertility and PCOS have made that wanting a long and difficult road. I've known since I was a teenager that carrying a child might not come easily, but the ache for motherhood has stayed with me, unwavering. It lingered through my 30s, growing sharper with time—etched deeper by fertility treatments, the endless rhythm of injections, and losses that still rest heavy in my bones.

For a time, it felt like we had everything. After all those years of waiting, Taylor was pregnant with our first child. We felt certain, our lives filled to the brim, poised to step into the future we had dreamed of.

I had tried to be happy for Taylor's healthy pregnancy, and I was. But it coexisted with envy and a hollow ache. But with my hand on her belly, feeling our baby move for the first time, the grief began to soften. I started to fall in love—not just with the baby we had wanted so desperately, but with Taylor in this

The Partner's Experience: Alison's Story

new phase of her parenthood, and with myself, too, as I became something more than her partner: a mother. Every night after that, I fell asleep with my hand on her belly, feeling for signs of life.

There's a photo from that time—me curled around her, one hand on her belly, the other holding her close. It looks serene. But we were in a hospital bed in an ICU. Taylor was 24 weeks pregnant and had just been diagnosed with a peach-sized malignant brain tumor. Our world collapsed almost instantly, and we were thrust into crisis. She had already lost the ability to read, write, and speak clearly. She was unsteady on her feet. Confused and disoriented. We didn't yet know that she would need urgent neurosurgery, followed by weeks of radiation and a year of grueling chemotherapy.

We met the NICU team within the first week of her diagnosis. Because the tumor was growing rapidly, surgery could not wait. There was no time to balance risks in favor of the pregnancy. The team came to her bedside and gently explained what might happen to our baby if she were born during the procedure. They prepared us for the best and worst possibilities. The discussion was matter-of-fact, and completely surreal.

After the brain surgery, we worked with Taylor's doctors to schedule a Cesarean section a few weeks later. The goal was to give our baby girl, whom we would later name Elliot, as much time as possible to grow, while not delaying Taylor's urgently needed radiation. The delivery date became a strategic calculation—a balance between the needs of parent and child.

By then, I'd let go of my vision of being Taylor's birth partner in the traditional sense. I'd imagined being her rock, her partner in birth. Instead, I found myself a quiet, masked observer in a sterile operating room, unsure of my place, my hands trembling inside a paper gown clearly sized for someone much larger. There was no script for this.

Balancing the roles of caregiver and expectant parent was never something I prepared for—it was something I learned to survive, moment by moment. It wasn't a balance at all—it was a collision. I was holding both at once: the tenderness of waiting for our daughter, and the urgency of fighting for Taylor's life. I had imagined preparing for parenthood with Taylor by my side, both of us focused on the baby we longed for. Instead, I found myself advocating for two lives at once—making medical decisions, managing appointments, and learning the language of neurology and neonatology in the same breath. I was learning how to mother and how to advocate in the same breath, with no pause for grief or rest. One moment I was helping Taylor as she recovered from massive brain surgery, the next I was listening to

The Partner's Experience: Alison's Story

NICU doctors explain what might happen when Elliot came too early.

I wanted to be present for the joy of pregnancy, for the small, sweet moments of anticipation, but they were always shadowed by the weight of Taylor's illness. I didn't know if Taylor would live to see Elliot born, speak our daughter's name, or hold her in the quiet safety of home.

I didn't get to just be excited. I didn't get to just be scared. I was both, all the time—learning to parent while also learning to let go of the life I thought we'd have. The joy of becoming a mother was braided tightly with fear, with exhaustion, with the relentless need to keep us all afloat.

At 32 weeks, Elliot was born tiny and struggling, but alive. When I saw her for the first time, I felt a terror unlike anything I'd ever known. But I didn't have time to collapse under its weight. I had to be steady. Present. Ready. For Elliot. For Taylor.

Taylor's bond with Elliot was instantaneous. She held her, and her whole body softened; the world stilled. It was beautiful to witness. And hard. Watching them fall in love was exquisite—and quietly painful. There was a visceral connection between them, one my body hadn't been part of. There was something unspoken that Taylor had gained in the act of giving birth—something primal. There was something that birth had given her that I didn't have.

My own bond with Elliot came slower. It wasn't sparked by biology but by action. I protected her. I advocated for her. I made decisions with her care team, updated family and friends, and navigated the long days in the NICU. I gave Taylor every second of precious skin-to-skin time in those early days and tried instead to hold the rest of it: the worry, the logistics, the relentless tasks.

I felt quietly isolated. Everyone asked how Elliot and Taylor were doing. No one asked about me. People told me I was strong, and that they could never handle what I was handling. But I wasn't strong—I was just surviving, doing what needed to be done because there was no other option.

Before Taylor's diagnosis, I had already planned to induce lactation. I thought it might help me connect with Elliot and ease the feeding load. After the diagnosis, it became necessary. I started pumping six weeks before her birth—12 times a day, 30 minutes each time. By the time she was born, I had a modest supply of milk and a small stash in the freezer.

The NICU team didn't quite know what to do with me. "No, I didn't give birth. Yes, the milk is mine." People asked questions: How did you force your body to make milk? Is that even safe? Is that real? And always, that qualifier: just. I was "just" lactating. "Just" the other parent.

The Partner's Experience: Alison's Story

I loved them more than I knew was possible. And still, I felt outside of it—watching instead of participating.

Because of Taylor's illness, neither of us was working. We spent every day in the NICU, arriving by 8 a.m. and staying until after Elliot's 9 p.m. care. We learned her schedule—every feeding, every diaper, every weigh-in. In between, we sat and watched. Her chest rising and falling. The numbers on the monitors flickering. The alarms were constant. Even when they weren't urgent, they sent a jolt through me.

And all of this—every step, every moment—unfolded in a medical system designed for heteronormative families. That truth was never far from view. These moments—misgenderings, assumptions, subtle exclusions—aren't rare. They're structural—built into a system that doesn't quite know where to place queer families, and that still sees us as exceptions instead of part of the norm.

Still, every day, we showed up. We fed our daughter. We held her. We learned her cues. We asked hard questions and made impossible choices. We created safety for each other in a space that didn't always know what to do with us.

That's the truth of queer parenting sometimes: It's not just the act of loving, it's the work of being seen as a family in a world that doesn't default to recognizing you as one. It's the repeated, quiet labor of correcting assumptions while you're still learning how to do it all yourself. It's love—and clarity—performed over and over in the face of uncertainty.

Bringing Elliot home happened both slower and faster than we expected. We had waited for weeks, counting the days, wondering when she would finally be ready. But when the doctors decided, it was immediate: One moment she was a NICU baby, the next she was in our arms, in our home, without monitors, without nurses, without backup. It was evening when we walked through the door, just the three of us, and I was terrified—terrified of getting it wrong, of missing some tiny but vital sign that she needed help, of not being able to feed her enough, of her slipping away from us without the safety net of machines to tell us she was okay.

And I was terrified, too, of how to care for both of them. How to strike the balance between letting Taylor care for Elliot—letting her mother in her own way—and knowing that her brain wasn't what it had been. She couldn't always remember, and couldn't always track, what Elliot needed or what she needed herself. I didn't want to take that from her, but I didn't know how to share it either.

All of this—the fear, the frustration, the constant effort—was wrapped in the knowledge that Taylor is dying. That this time she has with Elliot is limited. That whatever future I thought we would have, we won't. And that has changed everything. The things I thought would matter just don't. The sleep schedules, the baby books, the rules about self-soothing, and about putting her down "drowsy but awake"—none of it matters. All I want is for Taylor and Elliot to have each other for as long as they can. I want Elliot to know her mother's arms, to feel her heartbeat, to carry that with her when Taylor is gone.

Elliot's story didn't begin the way I had hoped. The NICU was a place of deep contradiction—both refuge and battleground, sanctuary and reminder. I was entrusted with our daughter's delicate care while also being reminded, in subtle and not-so-subtle ways, that our family didn't quite fit the mold. Intake forms left no space for two mothers. Questions that assumed a father would be arriving soon, and quiet pauses after I introduced myself. And yet, amid feeding tubes and oxygen monitors, we learned to live inside the rhythm of that place. We celebrated stabilized vitals and ounces gained. We learned to read monitors and nurses' expressions before they spoke. We whispered lullabies before rounds and carved out space for our love in the sterile choreography of care.

We didn't get the beginning I imagined, but in the long, quiet hours of the NICU—where time bent and progress was measured in heartbeats and feedings—we became a family. Not through ease, but through endurance. Not in spite of the system, but around it.

Our love didn't just show up—it expanded, stretched, and demanded space. That is where our story began.

What helped me, if I can even call it that, was finding the smallest spaces where I could be honest—where I didn't have to be strong or together or resilient. The quiet moments, even five minutes in a hospital hallway, where I could breathe and remember that I was still a person, not just a caretaker. A place to cry without apology. A place to tell the truth about how hard it all was. Reflection didn't always come in real time, but when it did, it let me soften just enough to keep going.

Community, too, held me up. Queer families, chosen family, the ones who didn't need a script to know how to show up, and my therapist, who met me virtually wherever I could find a sliver of privacy—even in tiny call rooms meant for overnight hospital staff—helped me to carve out space just to breathe. These people didn't fix it. They couldn't. But these moments of care, of showing up, were the thread that kept me tethered to those who love us, and to myself.

And writing—when I could—gave shape to what felt unshapable. I used an online resource to update our community, a place to keep everyone informed, to let them in. It offered a way to share, but it also asked for something from me—a kind of purposeful, relentless positivity, even when that felt false. The act of writing gave me something to hold onto—a thread

The Partner's Experience: Alison's Story

of connection, a way to mark the days. This book, this space, is part of that. A place where our stories, messy and real and fiercely tender, can live. If you're in the thick of it, I hope this gives you something to hold onto, even if it's just knowing that someone else has been there too.

Our story didn't start the way I had imagined, and it hasn't followed any path I would have chosen. And if you're reading this book, I imagine your story isn't going the way you planned either. But here we are. Still loving. Still holding on. Still finding ways to begin again. I've learned that love, especially queer love, knows how to make a life in even the harshest places. It expands. It insists. It holds. And so do we.

Section 1: The Beginning

This section includes questions relating to the very beginning of your NICU story. You already just navigated one life-changing experience—the birth of your baby, whether biologically or through surrogacy or adoption—and now, immediately, you've transitioned to another. It's hard to imagine how so many big things could be packed so closely together. That's a lot to hold. We're here to hold it with you as you slow down and remember.

Partners, remember: These questions are for everyone. If you have an answer to a question, even if it's not labeled "Partner Question," it's meant for you.

Your NICU Story

One

It's common for NICU families to feel the need for some degree of healing after their experience. Has that been the case for you? Prior to picking up this book, what steps have you taken and/or what tools have you used to begin processing your experience?

_____

_____

_____

_____

_____

_____

_____

_____

Section 1: The Beginning

Two

Where does your story start? Did you have any idea prior to your baby's or babies' birth that a NICU stay might be needed?

_____

_____

_____

_____

_____

_____

_____

_____

_____

_____

_____

Three

If they were present, what did it feel like to have the NICU team there when (or soon after) your baby was born?

Partner Question: Do you have any feelings or memories to process here related to your partner's birth experience? For example, were you scared that they might not survive?

_____

_____

_____

_____

_____

_____

_____

_____

Section 1: The Beginning

Four

Did your baby receive care close to where they were born, or did they need to be transferred/cared for somewhere else?

Five

Did you reach out to anyone to let them know your baby or babies would be admitted to the NICU? How long did you wait to do this? What was their reaction, and how did that feel to you?

Partner Question: Many times non-birthing partners feel solely responsible for being the point of contact for communication to family and friends. Was this your experience? How did that feel to you?

_____

_____

_____

_____

_____

_____

_____

Section 1: The Beginning

Other Thoughts

Your NICU Story

Other Thoughts

Other Thoughts

Your NICU Story

Take a breath. We're not rushing through, so if you need some time before continuing, please take it. Take some time to reach your arms up over your head, reheat your coffee, or feel a bit of fresh air on your face. Remember you are in control of the pacing of your reflection. Whether it's 15 minutes or 15 days, take the pause you need to move through these pages as it works for you.

When you're ready, turn the page to continue your NICU experience reflection.

Section 2: The Stay

This section offers guided prompts around your baby's or babies' stay in the NICU. Some questions may feel triggering and some may not feel relevant. All feelings are valid. Take what resonates with you and leave the rest. In the same way you're in control of the speed with which you move through this book, you are also in control of meeting your needs for things like space, quiet, or company.

Your NICU Story

One

Did you feel prepared for your baby's or babies' NICU stay? In which ways did you feel accepting, and in which ways did you feel caught off guard?

Two

What was the NICU environment like for you? What did it actually feel like to your physical body? Who else was around, and in what ways did they help this process (or not)?

Partner Question: Did it feel like you had permission to notice how things felt to your body? Sometimes partners feel that their attention needs to be on everyone but themselves.

_____

_____

_____

_____

_____

_____

_____

Your NICU Story

Three

What sounds, smells, tastes, or images come to mind when you think of the NICU environment? When you hear, smell, taste, or see them, what does it feel like in your body?

_____

_____

_____

_____

_____

_____

_____

_____

_____

_____

Section 2: The Stay

Four

For some parents, the rotation of providers can be challenging. How did the rotation of hospital staff impact you?

Did you work with one facility/care team, or did you transfer care?

Partner Question: Were you acknowledged by the care team in a way that felt supportive to you?

_____

_____

_____

_____

_____

_____

_____

Your NICU Story

Five

Many families get displaced if they do not live close to the NICU. Did you have to relocate? If so, what was that process like for you? What comes to mind when you think of having to relocate?

_____

_____

_____

_____

_____

_____

_____

_____

_____

_____

Section 2: The Stay

Six

A NICU stay is expensive. Did you feel financially supported throughout your experience? Which resources did you need but not have access to? What else could have made your financial experience go more smoothly?

Partner Question: Did you feel responsible for being the one to take care of family finances during your baby's stay?

_____

_____

_____

_____

_____

_____

_____

_____

Your NICU Story

Seven

NICU families are often inundated with medical information, and for many, it can be a lot to process. Who provided information to you? Who did you come to trust the most as an informant?

Which information was helpful and which was not? How did you sort that out?

_____

_____

_____

_____

_____

_____

_____

_____

Section 2: The Stay

Eight

Did you ever feel overwhelmed with the amount of information? If so, did you use any tools, like taking notes on your phone or recording voice memos, to make the information more accessible?

_____

_____

_____

_____

_____

_____

_____

_____

_____

Your NICU Story

Nine

For some, a community can be formed in the NICU. Did you connect with other babies' families while in the NICU? If so, did you find that helpful? If not, is that something you feel was missing?

Did you seek support from any organizations specializing in NICU support?

_____

_____

_____

_____

_____

_____

_____

Section 2: The Stay

Ten

Were there any providers with whom you had difficulty? How did you navigate that?

Eleven

What was your relationship with the hospital staff? Were there certain providers you connected with?

_____
_____
_____
_____
_____
_____
_____
_____
_____
_____
_____

Twelve

Balancing time among work, other children, and daily responsibilities can be overwhelming for families with a baby or babies in the NICU. What did you have to balance during your NICU stay? Were there parts of this that felt overwhelming or unmanageable?

Partner Question: If your partner remained hospitalized at the same time as your baby or babies, did you stay in the hospital with them, or did you need to take time to be at home?

_____

_____

_____

_____

_____

_____

_____

Thirteen

For many NICU families, their baby's well-being is the focus and, if one of the parents was the birthing person, their physical recovery is neglected. In what ways was your physical recovery neglected during the NICU stay? It's impossible to do and participate in all the healing processes without extra support.

Are there still ways your physical body is recovering?

Partner Question: Were there ways your well-being suffered as a result of focusing mainly on the needs of those around you? If so, in what ways? Are there any parts of your wellness that still need attention?

_____

_____

_____

_____

_____

_____

Section 2: The Stay

Fourteen

For many parents, a NICU stay often comes with uncertainty and questions such as whether and when their baby will come home.

Did you feel elements of uncertainty during your NICU stay? How did you navigate the uncertainty? When you think about the uncertainty, where do you feel it in your body?

_____

_____

_____

_____

_____

_____

_____

_____

Your NICU Story

Fifteen

In what ways did you feel your baby was well cared for? Are there ways you think their care may have been improved?

_____

_____

_____

_____

_____

_____

_____

_____

_____

Section 2: The Stay

Sixteen

In what ways did you feel your family was well cared for? Are there ways your family's care could have been improved?

_____

_____

_____

_____

_____

_____

_____

_____

_____

_____

Your NICU Story

Seventeen

Who in your life, if anyone, let you talk freely and openly about your experience? Who was the best listener?

_____

_____

_____

_____

_____

_____

_____

_____

_____

Section 2: The Stay

Eighteen

When your baby or babies were in the NICU, did you develop any routines that felt helpful or were necessary? This could look like getting coffee at a certain place each day, scrubbing your hands clean upon arrival, or singing a certain song to your baby whenever you held their hand.

_____

_____

_____

_____

_____

_____

_____

_____

Your NICU Story

Other Thoughts

Section 2: The Stay

Other Thoughts

Your NICU Story

Other Thoughts

Section 2: The Stay

You just worked through a lot of memories. Shake it out; relax your shoulders. The next section is an opportunity to reflect specifically on your relationship with your baby or babies while they were in the NICU.

Section 3: Your Baby

In this section, we ask questions that will help you reflect on what it was like to get to know your baby. A NICU stay isn't usually the way parents envision beginning their journey into parenthood or into their relationship with their baby. At all. We encourage you to be gentle with yourself as you consider how things were for you versus how you hoped they may have been. It's okay to recognize that there could be a big difference there. As with all of the other sections, take what resonates with you and leave the rest. There are extra pages at the end if you need more room to reflect.

There might be some questions in this section that feel more emotional or detailed than ones you've answered so far. You may find that you take longer to answer them or need more time in between responses.

Your NICU Story

One

What did you learn about yourself as a result of being with your baby or babies in the NICU? What did you learn about your baby or babies?

What strengths did you discover about yourself in the NICU? If a partner was present in your story, what did you discover about your partner or your loved ones?

_____

_____

_____

_____

_____

_____

_____

_____

Section 3: Your Baby

Two

What do you wish others knew about your baby's journey?

_____

_____

_____

_____

_____

_____

_____

_____

_____

_____

Your NICU Story

Three

What was it like seeing your baby or babies for the first time in the NICU?

_____

_____

_____

_____

_____

_____

_____

_____

_____

_____

Four

If machines and monitors were included in your baby's or babies' care, how did you feel when you saw your baby or babies hooked up to those?

_____

_____

_____

_____

_____

_____

_____

_____

_____

_____

Your NICU Story

Five

Did the NICU impact your ability to bond with your baby? In what way(s)?

_____
_____
_____
_____
_____
_____
_____
_____
_____
_____

Six

In what ways were you able to bond with your baby or babies while they were in the NICU? If you're feeling like the NICU impacted your ability to bond with your baby, know that many NICU families also have that experience. This space may assist with processing that.

Your NICU Story

Seven

Were there any moments when your little one surprised you with their strength or progress?

_____

_____

_____

_____

_____

_____

_____

_____

_____

_____

Eight

Were you able to hold your baby or babies right away, or did you have to wait? How did that feel? If you were unable to hold them, or chose not to, this space is for you to reflect on that, too.

_____

_____

_____

_____

_____

_____

_____

_____

_____

Your NICU Story

Nine

This is a space for you to write a letter to your baby or babies, if you'd like, about your experience with them in the NICU. What might you say to them?

_____

_____

_____

_____

_____

_____

_____

_____

_____

_____

Section 3: Your Baby

Other Thoughts

Your NICU Story

Other Thoughts

_____

_____

_____

_____

_____

_____

_____

_____

_____

_____

_____

_____

_____

Section 3: Your Baby

Other Thoughts

From here, you will either move to Section 4: Leaving Part of You Behind (for cases of infant loss) or Section 5: Going Home (for times when babies are discharged to home). Of course, you are welcome to complete both sections if they apply.

For those who left the NICU without their baby or babies, there may be grief that arises at this moment. We invite you to allow that grief, or whatever feelings arise, to be present.

Section 4: Leaving Part of You Behind

In this section, the prompts guide you through leaving the NICU without your baby. Be kind to yourself and take breaks when you need to. I (Mahaley) know the devastation that will be revisited throughout this section, and it is important to go at your own pace. In case it would be helpful to hear a bit about my process, I decided to share a bit here about what supported me in my grief.

Walking out of the NICU without my daughter in my arms was the most devastating moment of my life. It changed the fabric of who I am, and navigating my life after Saachi died has been incredibly complex.

Writing changed the landscape of my grief. It has

given me access to words and images and metaphors and language to color my grief. Most of all, it has given me dedicated time to spend with Saachi. In a PoliticsJOE interview about his book, *A Heart That Works,* actor Rob Delaney says that he has four children, and even though one of them is dead, they still all get roughly 25% of his parenting energy. Hearing him put that idea into words helped me realize that it is incredibly important for me to still actively parent Saachi. I believe in the power of language and writing, especially when navigating trauma and grief. I hope that these reflection prompts will be a safe space for you to color your grief as well as a positive step in your healing journey. Perhaps it will even be a way for you to spend time with your baby or babies. From one bereaved parent to another, I am profoundly sorry for your loss.

    With love and gratitude,
    Saachi's mom

Section 4: Leaving Part of You Behind

One

How did you feel walking out of the NICU without your baby?

_____

_____

_____

_____

_____

_____

_____

_____

_____

_____

Your NICU Story

Two

In what ways did your NICU care team acknowledge your loss of your baby? Which were the most impactful?

_____

_____

_____

_____

_____

_____

_____

_____

_____

Section 4: Leaving Part of You Behind

Three

Were there any meaningful rituals or acknowledgments, such as a keepsake or memory box from the hospital, that helped you feel supported or seen at the end of your NICU stay?

_____

_____

_____

_____

_____

_____

_____

_____

_____

Your NICU Story

Four

There can often be a lot of support while families are in the NICU, whether from friends, family members, and/or staff. Did you feel supported coming home? Who did you feel supported by? Was there anyone you did not feel support from?

_____

_____

_____

_____

_____

_____

_____

_____

_____

Section 4: Leaving Part of You Behind

Five

Did any friends or family members help you feel especially "seen" in your grief? How so?

_____

_____

_____

_____

_____

_____

_____

_____

_____

_____

_____

Six

What were the biggest challenges of the time you spent in the NICU?

_____

_____

_____

_____

_____

_____

_____

_____

_____

_____

_____

Section 4: Leaving Part of You Behind

Seven

Notice what, if anything, might need to be forgiven specifically around the time spent in the NICU. Some parents hold a sense of responsibility about things they could have done differently. What, if anything, do you feel responsible for regarding your baby's NICU stay? Where do you feel that in your body? What, if anything, needs to be forgiven?

Some parents may have some feelings, such as anger or resentment, toward a situation or even a provider. What's present for you? Is any amount of this ready to be forgiven? Sometimes forgiveness happens in degrees, not all at once.

Now could be a time when taking a stretch break or getting some fresh air might feel good. You can use this reminder as a brief check-in with your physical and emotional needs as well.

_____

_____

_____

_____

Your NICU Story

Eight

Are there certain sounds, smells, physical items, or other triggers that still remind you of the NICU? If so, what are they?

_____

_____

_____

_____

_____

_____

_____

_____

_____

Section 4: Leaving Part of You Behind

Nine

What were the biggest unexpected positives/gifts that came from spending time in the NICU?

_____

_____

_____

_____

_____

_____

_____

_____

_____

_____

Your NICU Story

Ten

If there were providers you connected with during your stay, how did it feel to not see them regularly anymore?

_____

_____

_____

_____

_____

_____

_____

_____

_____

Section 4: Leaving Part of You Behind

Eleven

If a partner was present in your story, how did this experience change your relationship with them?

_____

_____

_____

_____

_____

_____

_____

_____

_____

_____

Twelve

How did this experience change your outlook on life?

_____

_____

_____

_____

_____

_____

_____

_____

_____

_____

Section 4: Leaving Part of You Behind

Thirteen

What would you say to another parent who is experiencing or has experienced loss in the NICU?

_____

_____

_____

_____

_____

_____

_____

_____

_____

_____

_____

Fourteen

When you think about the memories of your NICU experience, where do you feel them in your body? For example, perhaps your chest tightens when you hear a "beep" noise that reminds you of a machine sound.

_____

_____

_____

_____

_____

_____

_____

_____

_____

_____

Section 4: Leaving Part of You Behind

Other Thoughts

_____

_____

_____

_____

_____

_____

_____

_____

_____

_____

_____

_____

_____

Your NICU Story

Other Thoughts

_____

_____

_____

_____

_____

_____

_____

_____

_____

_____

_____

_____

_____

Section 4: Leaving Part of You Behind

Other Thoughts

Losing your baby in the NICU is one of the hardest experiences a parent can face, and there is no right or wrong way to grieve. In fact, in some ways it felt difficult writing a conclusion to this section because there is no way to wrap up neatly and make it hurt less. Be gentle with yourself as you navigate this overwhelming journey. You may feel a mix of emotions—grief, love, anger, numbness, or anything else—and all of these feelings are valid.

Your baby's life, however brief, mattered deeply. Their presence has left a lasting imprint on your heart and your story. Hold onto the moments you shared, and let yourself feel whatever you need to feel as you take this journey one step at a time.

Your grief is not forgotten, and neither is your baby. You are part of a community of parents who understand your pain and honor your strength. Please remember that healing doesn't mean forgetting—it means carrying your baby's memory forward in your own unique way.

You are loved, and your grief is seen.

Section 5: Going Home

A NICU stay can feel like the longest wait in the world. You're so ready to be home, and also perhaps feeling apprehensive about being "on your own" without medical providers to help care for your little one(s). And then there's the waiting for all the milestones to be met so your baby or babies can be discharged,* as well as the learning or planning of logistics in case your baby or babies are being discharged with special equipment.

*We recognize if you had multiple babies receiving care in the NICU, they may not have been discharged at the same time, or perhaps had different endings to their NICU stories.

Your NICU Story

One

How did you feel walking out of the NICU with your baby?

_____

_____

_____

_____

_____

_____

_____

_____

_____

_____

Section 5: Going Home

Two

For many parents, the constant monitoring in the NICU can be comforting. What was it like to come home and have less monitoring on your baby?

_____
_____
_____
_____
_____
_____
_____
_____
_____
_____

Your NICU Story

Three

If your baby came home with medical equipment, how did that shape your transition home from the hospital? What challenges did you have, if any, using the equipment at home?

_____

_____

_____

_____

_____

_____

_____

_____

_____

Section 5: Going Home

Four

There can often be a lot of support while families are in the NICU, whether from friends, family members, and/or staff. Did you feel supported coming home? Who did you feel supported by? Was there anyone you did not feel support from?

Partner Question: Did you feel like you were allowed to ask for support as a non-birthing parent?

_____

_____

_____

_____

_____

_____

_____

_____

Your NICU Story

Five

What is a memory you have of feeling loved by your family or community after you got home?

_____

_____

_____

_____

_____

_____

_____

_____

_____

_____

_____

Six

At what point did you start feeling settled at home? What would have allowed you to feel settled sooner?

_____

_____

_____

_____

_____

_____

_____

_____

_____

_____

_____

_____

Your NICU Story

Seven

What were the biggest challenges of spending time in the NICU?

Eight

Notice what, if anything, might need to be forgiven specifically around the time spent in the NICU. Some parents hold a sense of responsibility about things they could have done differently. What, if anything, do you feel responsible for regarding your baby's NICU stay? Where do you feel that in your body? What, if anything, needs to be forgiven?

Some parents may have some feelings, such as anger or resentment, toward a situation or even a provider. What's present for you? Is any amount of this ready to be forgiven? Sometimes forgiveness happens in degrees, not all at once.

Now could be a time when taking a stretch break or getting some fresh air might feel good. You can use this reminder as a brief check-in with your physical and emotional needs as well.

_____

_____

_____

_____

Your NICU Story

Nine

Are there certain sounds, smells, physical items, or other triggers that still remind you of the NICU? If so, what are they?

_____

_____

_____

_____

_____

_____

_____

_____

_____

Section 5: Going Home

Ten

What were the biggest unexpected positives/gifts that came from spending time in the NICU?

Eleven

If there were providers you connected with during your stay, how did (or does) it feel to not see them regularly anymore?

Twelve

If a partner was present in your story, how did this experience change your relationship with them?

_____

_____

_____

_____

_____

_____

_____

_____

_____

_____

_____

Your NICU Story

Thirteen

How did this experience change your outlook on life?

_____

_____

_____

_____

_____

_____

_____

_____

_____

Fourteen

What would you say to another parent who is experiencing or has experienced a NICU stay?

_____

_____

_____

_____

_____

_____

_____

_____

_____

_____

_____

_____

Fifteen

When you think about the memories of your NICU experience, where do you feel them in your body? For example, perhaps your chest tightens when you hear a "beep" noise that reminds you of a machine sound.

_____

_____

_____

_____

_____

_____

_____

_____

_____

_____

Section 5: Going Home

Your NICU story isn't over when you walk out of the NICU. As you have probably learned, that story lives within you, even after you see your baby growing and becoming themselves. Even after you have spent time with your story using this guide, big feelings may flare up at what feels like an inopportune time. This is typical after experiencing upsetting memories or trauma related to a NICU stay. Think of this emergence of a feeling or memory as an invitation for attention. It's okay to make room for your story's energy to wax and wane. It might feel very loud at some times, and quiet at others. When it is loud, see if it might be asking for some space to be heard.

For example, is there something you'd like to journal about? Would it feel good to place a hand over your heart and breathe compassion into the tender part of you that holds the story? Or does your past self need to hear that you're in the present, and your baby is safe? Whatever that part of you needs, see if you might be able to notice it with acceptance. And it's okay if you don't get it perfect. As a reminder, we've included a "Resources" page at the end of the book in case you're feeling like you would benefit from some additional support.

Thank you so much for walking through this journey with us. We know it can be hard, at times, to revisit such a challenging time in your life. We hope you found value in expanding your story to include all of its parts—the tough and the amazing.

Your NICU Story

Other Thoughts

_____

_____

_____

_____

_____

_____

_____

_____

_____

_____

_____

_____

_____

Section 5: Going Home

Other Thoughts

Your NICU Story

Other Thoughts

Resources

Postpartum Support International
www.postpartum.net

For NICU Support:

Dear NICU Mama
https://www.dearnicumama.com/

Hand to Hold
https://handtohold.org/

March of Dimes NICU Family Support®
https://www.marchofdimes.org/our-work/nicu-family-support

NICU Parent Network
https://nicuparentnetwork.org/

Your NICU Story

For Infant Loss:

RTZ Hope
https://rtzhope.org/

Stillborn and Infant Loss Support (SAILS)
https://www.bornintosilence.org/

The TEARS Foundation
https://thetearsfoundation.org/

Forever Footprints
https://foreverfootprints.org/

Acknowledgments

We had the most incredible team involved in this process with us! We would like to thank:

Ravi: You brought such a captivating story to our readers, and we are so grateful. The way you seamlessly weave humor into the reality of your stress and grief is an art. It's incredibly inspiring. Thanks so much for sharing that here.

Alison: Thank you for taking a chance on us and sharing your story with our readers! You are a beautiful writer, and the way you tell your family's story instantly forms a connection with anyone reading your piece. We are so grateful for your share.

Beta Readers: Ana, Galadriel, Jessie, John, Kara, Kayla, Rachel, and Trey
We are so thankful you took time out of your busy lives to read our book and share your honest thoughts with us. We know you all had different NICU experiences and outcomes, and it means the world to

us that you were willing to explore painful memories to help make this book the best version it could be.

Editing: Jodi, thank you for taking our draft and making it book-ready! We know how valuable it was to have your eye on things to help us connect with our readers in the way we hoped.

Design: Jess, thank you for hearing our vision for the book design and curating a beautiful cover and layout. You have such a gift for designing!

PR: Jessica, your support has been indispensable for us during the process of introducing our book to the world! Your expert guidance and planning showed us exactly what to do to start spreading the word about *Your NICU Story*.

Mahaley
I would like to start off by saying thank you to Emily for responding to an email from a stranger asking her to write a book together. This process has been wildly meaningful and I am so grateful to now call you a friend through it all.

Community is incredibly important to me and this book would have never come to fruition without the encouragement from my friends and family to write. Savannah, who gave a journal and a pen after Saachi

Acknowledgments

died. Kara, who has helped me find my way each and every day after Saachi died—to know you is the gift of a lifetime. To my parents, closest friends, and in-laws, thank you for always encouraging me to share about Saachi and to keep writing. And to our incredible village of caregivers who love on my children so I can work, thank you for giving me space to help others and to spend time with Saachi.

To Saachi's care team at Monroe Carell Jr. Children's Hospital at Vanderbilt, I am in deep gratitude for all the care and effort you gave to save my daughter. You all treated us and Saachi with such love and tenderness. We are forever grateful to all of you.

My husband, Ravi, for always making space in the chaos for me to pursue my dreams. You are the love of my life and the definition of a true partner. In any other lifetime, I would still choose you. To my daughter Amelie—my greatest teacher—you are the reason I kept going. To my rainbows, Kaaya and Archi, thank you for a second chance at life. And to my daughter Saachi, being your mom is the greatest gift I have ever been given. You continue to spread your magic throughout the world and it is the honor and joy of my life to witness it.

Emily
The universe works in truly fun and magical ways

(and also mysterious and painful ones at times, but I digress). I was so tickled to get a message from Mahaley asking to work together and was incredibly touched that she reached out to me. Mahaley, I have so enjoyed developing this friendship with you! What an awesome way to connect and collaborate. The way you continue a relationship with Saachi is inspiring and beautiful.

Writing projects have a way of taking time away from other parts of your life! I wouldn't trade it for anything, and I am also deeply grateful to my family for their patience and support. To my kids, Wyatt and Lillie, for continually teaching me how to be flexible and prioritize connection. To my husband, Mike, for still breaking into hysterical laughter with me over the silliest things; having that stress release is invaluable. I also want to extend gratitude and huge hugs to many of my dear friends for listening while I talked about this project through all of its stages and for giving me confidence boosts when needed.

About the Authors

Mahaley Patel, LMFT, PMH-C, is a licensed therapist specializing in perinatal mental health, grief, trauma, and infant/child loss. She serves on the bereaved parent advisory board Monroe Carell Jr. Children's Hospital at Vanderbilt, and runs a child loss support group for grieving parents. She holds a bachelor of arts from UCLA and a master's degree from Pepperdine University.

Mahaley and her family live in Nashville, Tennessee. She is a wife, a mom to four humans and two cats, and a bereaved parent.

Learn more at www.mahaleypatel.com.

Emily Souder, LCSW-C, PMH-C, is a licensed therapist certified in perinatal mental health with master's degrees in applied sociology and social work. She and her family live in Maryland, homeschooling and exploring, and getting curious about life. Emily loves tea, finding mushrooms in the woods, and drawing amusement from wherever she can.

Emily has written multiple books, including *Birth Story Brave, Reimagined: A Guide for Reflecting on Your Childbirth Experience*; *Birth Story Held for Loss: A Guide for Reflecting on Your Fertility Experience, Miscarriage, Abortion, TFMR, Stillbirth, and Infant Loss*; and *Sparks: Inspiration for Extinguishing the Power of Fear and Igniting Amusement, Knowing, and Trust*.

Learn more at www.emilysouder.com.

www.ingramcontent.com/pod-product-compliance
Lightning Source LLC
Chambersburg PA
CBHW052144070526
44585CB00017B/1975